EDGE BOOKS™

LIBRARY OF WEIRD

THE WORLD'S
ODDEST
INVENTIONS

by Nadia Higgins

CAPSTONE PRESS
a capstone imprint

Edge Books are published by Capstone Press,
1710 Roe Crest Drive, North Mankato, Minnesota 56003.
www.capstonepub.com

Library of Congress Cataloging-in-Publication Data
Higgins, Nadia, author.
The world's oddest inventions / by Nadia Higgins.
pages cm.—(Edge books. Library of weird)
Summary: "Describes some of the oddest, strangest, and most bizarre inventions
from around the world"—Provided by publisher.
Audience: 8–12.
Audience: Grades 4 to 6.
Includes bibliographical references and index.
ISBN 978-1-4914-2016-4 (library binding)
ISBN 978-1-4914-2187-1 (ebook PDF)
1. Inventions—Juvenile literature. 2. Inventions—Miscellanea—Juvenile literature.
I. Title.
T15.H54 2015
600—dc23   2014014017

Editorial Credits
Aaron Sautter, editor; Kyle Grenz, designer; Charmaine Whitman and Katy
LaVigne, production designers; Pam Mitsakos, media researcher; Kathy McColley,
production specialist

Photo Credits
Alamy: marc macdonald, 18, Motoring Picture Library, 17, ZUMA Press, Inc., 11;
AP Images: ASSOCIATED PRESS, 23; Getty Images: Premium Archive/Nathan
Lazarnick/George Eastman House, 21, Getty Images Entertainment/Astrid
Stawiarz, 14, Archive Photos/FPG, 19, Hulton Archive/Fox Photos, 28, Photodisc,
29 (bottom), The Washington Post via Getty Images/Matt McClain, 10; Mary Evans:
Nationaal Archief/Spaarnestad Photo/Het Leven, 9; Newscom: Better Than Pants/
Splash, 27, Solent News/Splash News, 13, Splash News, 24, 29 (top), WENN.com/
ZOB/BB2, cover, WENN.com/CB2/ZOB, 7, WENN/TyneNews/TN1/ZOB, 15;
Shutterstock: MO_SES Premium, 8, back cover, James Steidl, 4–5; Science Source:
Photo Researchers, Inc., 25

Design Elements
Shutterstock: AridOcean, KID_A (throughout)

Printed in the United States of America in Stevens Point, Wisconsin.
092014   008479WZS15

TABLE OF CONTENTS

WEIRD AND WONDERFUL
INVENTIONS

What's the difference between a great invention and a ridiculous idea? It's hard to say. In 1876 people laughed at Alexander Graham Bell's new telephone. In the early 1900s people snickered at those goofy "horseless carriages" that slowly sputtered down the road. And in the 1940s many people thought that TVs were a passing fad. But cars, telephones, and TVs have all been incredibly successful inventions.

However, the odds of an invention succeeding aren't very good. Inventors have tried many wacky ideas throughout history. Each year governments give hundreds of thousands of **patents** to inventors. But 99 percent of inventors' ideas never actually make a profit.

patent—*a legal document giving someone sole rights to make or sell a product*

4

EARLY CAR, OR "HORSELESS CARRIAGE," FROM 1910

The great scientist and mathematician Albert Einstein once said, "If at first an idea is not absurd, then there is no hope for it." See how some people have taken Einstein's words to heart in the weirdest ways.

CHAPTER 1
WEARABLE WACKINESS

Why bother learning how to tie a tie when you can wear one that zips up instead? Or how would you like to wear a T-shirt that lets you play guitar? You never know what kind of wacky wearable invention will be the next big thing.

SMITTENS

One chilly day inventor Wendy Feller was going for a stroll with her husband. They tried to hold hands, but their bulky mittens ruined the romantic mood. That's when Wendy got the idea for Smittens. The **slogan** for these mittens for two says it all, "Hold hands. Stay warm. Love." Now sweethearts can stay inseparable, even in the coldest temperatures.

slogan—a phrase or motto used by a business, a group, or an individual

SOUND PERFUME GLASSES

Researchers in Japan want to help people's social life through eyewear. Sound Perfume glasses give off special scents and sounds when you meet new people. The glasses are meant to help you remember people's names. However, to work correctly, other people need to wear the glasses too.

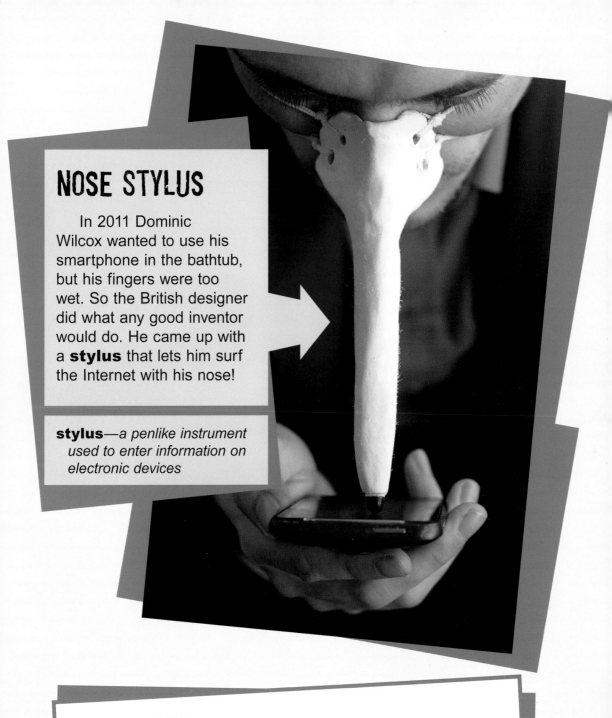

NOSE STYLUS

In 2011 Dominic Wilcox wanted to use his smartphone in the bathtub, but his fingers were too wet. So the British designer did what any good inventor would do. He came up with a **stylus** that lets him surf the Internet with his nose!

stylus—*a penlike instrument used to enter information on electronic devices*

THE ZIPTIE

This "revolutionary" tie zips up just like a jacket. Other ties also use zippers but hide them behind a knot. However, the ZipTie turns the zipper itself into a fashion statement!

TEMPORARY LIP TATTOOS

Want leopard-print lips? Temporary lip tattoos come in a variety of patterns. Choose from rainbows, polka dots, American flags, and more! These funky temporary lip tattoos work like stickers. They go on with water and can be removed with baby oil.

GAZE-ACTIVATED DRESSES

Designer Ying Gao's high-tech dresses demand to be looked at—literally. Eye-tracking technology inside the fabric sets off tiny motors that make the dresses wave and wiggle when people look at them. The more people stare, the more the dresses squirm.

WOODEN BATHING SUITS

Roll out the barrels! In 1929 some people actually wore bathing suits made from wood. The suits supposedly helped people float in the water—if they could put up with the splinters!

SNOWSTORM FACE PROTECTORS

In the 1930s people braved blizzards with heavy coats and thick wool scarves. But the scarves could be very itchy. In 1939 someone tried to solve this problem with plastic snowstorm face protectors. People could watch as snowflakes slid right off the see-through cone. It worked well, until people's breath fogged it up—or they ran out of air!

ELECTRONIC GUITAR SHIRT

The guitar graphic on this T-shirt is actually playable! Buttons along the neck play major chords. To "strum" the guitar, just rub a coin across the bottom. This amazing invention even comes with a mini **amplifier** so everyone can hear you playing your shirt.

EYE SCREENS

Imagine what it would be like to read texts right on your eyeballs! A Belgian researcher is working to develop "smart" contact lenses that include built-in screens. These special lenses could someday be used as sunglasses, to read private messages, or even change people's eye color.

AMAZINGLY REALISTIC FACE MASKS

Next Halloween you can creep out your friends by going—as yourself! For about $4,000 a Japanese company can make a mask of your face that's incredibly lifelike. It even simulates the blood vessels inside your eyes. The mask combines photos of you from every angle, and then stretches the image over a 3-D mold of your face.

ELECTRIC FACIAL MASK

"Rejuvenique" was a real hit in the late 1990s. Makers of the battery-powered mask claimed that people could have more youthful looking skin. Tiny electrical shocks supposedly worked to tone facial muscles under the skin. But the truly shocking part was that the mask looked very creepy!

CHAPTER 2

HIGH-TECH HEAD SCRATCHERS

Successful inventions usually solve a problem or meet a need. But some inventions do odd things, such as putting designs on toast or letting dogs send text messages. Some inventions show that just because people can do something doesn't always mean they should.

DIGITAL TATTOOS

People can now get tattoos that change with the wave of a wand! A plastic surgeon first places a digital "canvas" under a person's skin. The user can then change the display at any time with computer software and a special electronic "wand." For example, people can change their body art from a skull to a heart in just a few seconds.

EYE-TRACKING CAMERA

The IRIS camera by designer Mimi Zou doesn't have any buttons. The camera is instead controlled only with your eyes. Just focus the camera by looking through it. You can zoom in or out by squinting or opening your eyes wide. Then blink twice to take a picture!

SCAN TOASTER

Here's a new way to have fun in the morning. The Scan Toaster first connects to your computer to get images of text or photos. Rotating wires inside the device then burn the images onto your morning toast. Now you can eat the news after you've finished reading it!

DIET FORK

Many people believe that eating food more slowly can help with weight loss. The HAPIfork can help people do just that. This electronic utensil counts your "fork servings" per minute. When people start scarfing down their dinner too fast, HAPIfork starts flashing and vibrating to let them know to slow down.

Electronic dog tag sends messages to your home computer, then Tweets to you!

PUPPY TWEETS

Imagine your phone buzzing you with the message, "I bark because I miss you." Now thanks to Puppy Tweets™, your dog can send you messages while you're away! An electronic tag on your dog's collar picks up certain sounds and movements made by your pet. The tag then sends one of 500 adorable messages to your dog's own Twitter feed.

REMOTE ANIMAL PETTER

Would you like to pet your dog while you're at school? You may soon be able to. Researchers at the National University of Singapore are using chickens to test a "tele-petting" system. First, someone pets a chicken-shaped doll that contains several touch sensors. The sensors then send signals over the Internet to a special jacket worn by a real chicken. The jacket recreates the person's touch so the chicken can feel it!

TRICKED-OUT TOILETS

If you have a boring, regular toilet, you don't know what you're missing. Just imagine relaxing to mood lighting in seven colors, foot warmers, music, and deodorizers. The high-tech Numi toilet has it all. It even has a built-in **bidet** to help you feel extra fresh!

bidet—*a low, sinklike bathroom fixture with a faucet that points up; a bidet is used to wash a person's bottom area*

"CLOCKY"

This wheeled alarm clock rolls away from you to make sure you roll out of bed. It beeps like a robot and can roll off of a 3-foot (0.9-meter) high surface. You never know which way it'll go, so you have to get up and look for it.

CHAPTER 3
ODD ON THE MOVE

Ready ... set ... pedal in the air! Jog on the water! Float across a continent! Throughout history people have looked for new ways to get from one place to another—and we're still at it. Welcome to the awesome oddness of inventions on the move.

AMPHIBIOUS BICYCLE

In 1975 India's Mohammed Saidullah got tired of his village being flooded every year. So he built a bicycle that he could ride both on land and in water. He added floats to the bike and put fan blades on the spokes—and it worked! Saidullah won several awards for his **ingenious** invention. However, he has yet to make any money from it.

ingenious—*inventive and original*

SEA JOGGER

Now you can walk on water with the Sea Jogger. First, hold the handlebars and step onto the springy surface. Then start walking in place to move the flippers underneath. If all goes well, you can walk across a nearby lake—and stay dry enough to keep your shoes on.

ICEBERG AIRCRAFT CARRIER

During World War II (1939–1945) British scientist Geoffrey Pyke had the idea of making an aircraft carrier out of pykrete. This incredibly tough material is made by freezing a mixture of wood pulp and water. The British government approved Pyke's idea and planned to build several pykrete ships. But the project proved to be too expensive and the plan was scrapped.

WORLD'S SMALLEST CAR

The British Peel P50 is the world's smallest street-legal car. It is also one of the rarest vehicles in the world. Only 50 of these tiny cars were built in the 1960s, and just 27 still exist today. They have three wheels, one door, and a small electric engine. At only 130 pounds (59 kilograms), a person can pull along the Peel P50 like a giant suitcase.

"HUMAN SPIDER-MAN" CLIMBING MACHINE

Some vacuum cleaners are more powerful than you might think. In 2010 British inventor Jem Stansfield attached vacuum cleaner hoses to two giant suction pads. Then he proceeded to climb up the side of a building—just like a certain wall-crawling superhero!

HUMAN-POWERED HELICOPTER

In 1980 the American Helicopter Society issued a challenge to engineers around the world. The first team to invent a human-powered machine that could fly 3 meters (9.8 feet) high for at least one minute would win $250,000. In June 2013 a team of Canadian engineers finally nabbed the prize. Their Atlas helicopter was powered by a bike that spun four giant **propellers**.

propeller—a set of rotating blades that moves a vehicle through water or air

VACUUM-TUBE TRAINS

Scientists are currently working on technology that will allow trains to travel seven times faster than commercial jet airplanes. Using magnets and **vacuum tubes**, the trains would float through airless tubes at up to 4,000 miles (6,440 km) per hour. There would be no wind, train tracks, or road to slow down the trains. However, safety concerns and the sky-high cost of building the train system are putting the brakes on this amazing idea.

vacuum tube—a tube that has no air or other matter in it

MONOWHEEL

In 1869 French inventor Rousseau of Marseilles created one of the world's first monowheels. Riders in these vehicles roll along inside a single large wheel. Monowheels supposedly offer a smoother ride than regular two-wheeled bikes. Over the years there have been many different monowheel designs. However, these vehicles are difficult to control and can crash easily.

ROLLER SUIT

Who says roller skates are just for feet? This suit of "rolling armor" features wheels attached to a person's feet, toes, elbows, knees, and more. Now you can pretend to "fly" like your favorite superhero as you roll down the street!

FACE-TO-FACE BIKE

This two-person bike has rotating seats and gears that can move in either direction. Two friends can ride sitting either face-to-face or back-to-back. But whichever way people are facing, the bike can still move forward.

THE REEVES OCTOAUTO

Car designers have tinkered with different designs since cars were first invented. In 1911 Milton Reeves had an idea for a new kind of car. He got out his welding torch and added four extra wheels to an Overland automobile. Reeves claimed the OctoAuto offered a smoother ride than regular cars. However, the eight-wheeled car handled corners terribly.

HORSEY HORSELESS CARRIAGE

In 1899 most people traveled in horse-drawn carriages. Cars, known then as "horseless carriages," were often a startling sight—especially for horses. But inventor Uriah Smith's Horsey Horseless vehicle was meant to solve that problem. Smith planned to place a wooden horse head on the front of a car. He thought the fake horse head would help soothe the nerves of real horses. Smith received a U.S. patent for his idea in 1899. However, it's not known if he ever got around to actually building this crazy car.

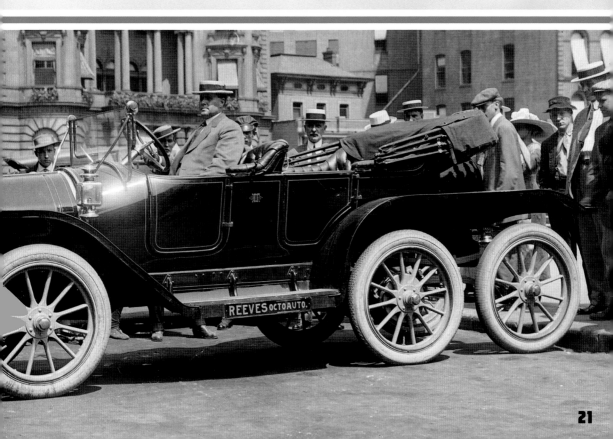

CHAPTER 4

HOW LAZY CAN YOU BE?

Without washing machines people today would still be scrubbing clothes by hand. Without the Internet people would have to spend hundreds of hours digging for information in books. Here are some other ways inventors have tried to save people time and make chores easier.

SIX-SECOND TOOTHBRUSH

The Blizzident toothbrush is unique to each person. This custom-made mouthpiece has 800 bristles sitting at perfect angles to fit your pearly whites. Bite and grind it between your teeth 10 to 15 times, and you're done brushing in just six seconds!

DEODORANT CANDY

Why bother putting on deodorant? Just eat some candy instead! According to the company that makes Deo Perfume Candy, eating just two to four pieces will keep you smelling rosy for up to six hours. The more you sweat, the better you'll smell!

BABY-PATTING MACHINE

It can take hours to get a baby to go to sleep. Luckily, babies are easy to trick. At least that's the idea behind this machine from a 1968 patent. A motor-driven arm would gently pat a baby's bottom until it fell asleep, freeing parents to relax or focus on other activities.

BRUSH AND SHINE

To brush or to shine? That is the question—at least for some balding men. In the 1950s one company invented a special grooming tool to do both! It brushed a man's hair on the sides of his head while shining the bald part on top at the same time.

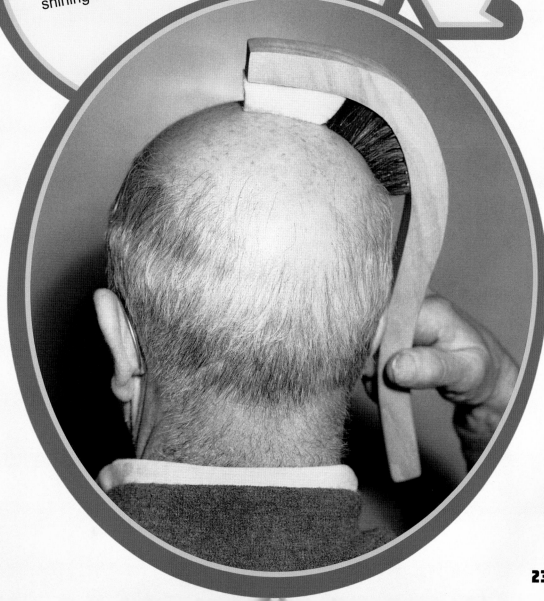

BOTANICALLS

Plants are a great way to add greenery to your home. But it's easy to forget about watering them. Now your plants can let you know when they're thirsty! The Botanicalls kit includes sensors to measure the moisture in your plant's pot. When the soil gets too dry, it sends a message to your phone: "Water me please." After watering your plant, you'll get a nice thank-you message as well.

SNOWBALL MAKER

The Sno-Baller gently packs snow into perfect snowballs. This snow scooper can supposedly form up to 60 snowballs per minute. As an added bonus, your hands don't even get cold or wet.

SELF-TIPPING HAT

In the late 1800s a proper gentleman always tipped his hat to a lady. But what if his arms were full? James C. Boyle solved this problem with a wind-up device worn under a man's hat. It could make any hat tip itself with just a nod of the wearer's head.

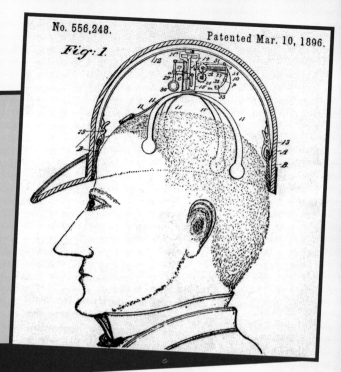

No. 556,248.   Patented Mar. 10, 1896.
Fig. 1

SELF-STIRRING MUG

This cool gadget lets you stir your drink without hunting for a spoon. The Self-Stirring Mug has a tiny plastic disc at the bottom. Just press the button to spin the disk and swirl your drink. You can even use the swirl feature to clean the mug with soapy water when you're done.

LAZYGLASSES

Want to lie flat on your back to watch TV or read a book? You don't have to install a screen on the ceiling. Just use Lazyglasses. These clever glasses use mirrors to reflect images to your eyes the same way **periscopes** do.

periscope—*a viewing device with mirrors at each end; periscopes are often used in submarines to see above water*

CHAPTER 5

STRANGE INVENTIONS JUST FOR KIDS

Some inventors seem to remember that being a kid means having fun. Invent some slimy goop to play with in the bathtub? That's awesome! But some inventions haven't been as much fun, such as a special brush for cleaning kids' necks. Which of the following inventions would earn your seal of approval?

NECK BRUSH COLLAR

Ouch! This plastic collar brush from 1950 was meant to clean a child's neck while he or she played. No soap or water was required. The brush worked completely dry—unless, of course, you count the kids' tears.

BABY MOP

In the late 1990s the Baby Mop started as a **spoof** advertisement in Japan. But today parents can actually buy fringed outfits that turn their babies into cleaning tools! Apparently hairballs and dust stick even better to crawling babies than to regular mops.

spoof—a funny imitation of something

X-RAY SHOE FITTER

What was the best way for people to get a good pair of shoes In the 1950s? By X-raying their own feet of course! Shoe-fitting fluoroscopes allowed shoppers to view the bones in their feet glowing inside their shoes. The machines supposedly tested people's feet to get the best fitting shoes. But as it turns out, the machines were a total **gimmick** and exposed people to cancer-causing radiation. Most of the machines were banned by 1970.

gimmick—*a clever trick or idea used to get people's attention*

GELLI BAFF

Bubble baths? How boring. Now parents can make bath time more fun with Gelli Baff! Sprinkle in a packet of "goo maker" and kids' bathwater turns into colorful, super-fun goop. When bathtime is done, just mix in some "goo dissolver." The slime turns to colored water that swirls down the drain.

BABY CAGE

City apartments can be awfully cramped with a baby around. This was especially true in the early 1900s. In 1922 inventor Emma Read created an original solution to this problem. She invented a mesh cage for babies that was literally stuck outside a window. The cage even came with a detachable, slanted roof that helped keep rain off the baby's head!

ANTI-THEFT LUNCH BAGS

Having trouble with people stealing your lunch? Here's a way to make sure they never steal your food again. These clever bags make a sandwich look moldy and gross so nobody will want to touch it. Just make sure nobody throws it away by accident!

INVENTING SUCCESS

Have you ever had an idea for an invention? Was it so strange that you thought people might laugh at you? If so, you're off to a good start! Don't let the slim chance of success get you down. Remember that many of the most successful inventions began as wonderfully weird and wacky ideas!

GLOSSARY

amplifier (AM-pluh-fy-uhr)—a piece of equipment that changes sound or makes it louder

bidet (bih-DAY)—a low, sinklike bathroom fixture with a faucet that points up; a bidet is used to wash a person's bottom area

gimmick (GIM-ik)—a clever trick or idea used to get people's attention

ingenious (in-JEEN-yuhss)—inventive and original

patent (PAT-uhnt)—a legal document giving someone sole rights to make or sell a product

periscope (PEHR-uh-skope)—a viewing device with mirrors at each end; periscopes are often used in submarines to see above water

propeller (pruh-PEL-ur)—a set of rotating blades that moves a vehicle through water or air

slogan (SLOH-guhn)—a phrase or motto used by a business, a group, or an individual

spoof (SPOOF)—a funny imitation of something

stylus (STY-luhs)—a penlike instrument used to enter information on electronic devices

vacuum tube (VAK-yoom TOOB)—a tube that has no air or other matter in it

READ MORE

Marsico, Katie. *Stinky Sanitation Inventions.* Awesome Inventions You Use Every Day. Minneapolis: Lerner Publications Company, 2014.

Ringstad, Arnold. *Weird-but-True Facts About Inventions.* Mankato, Minn.: Child's World, 2013.

Turner, Tracey. *100 Inventions That Made History: Brilliant Breakthroughs that Shaped Our World.* New York: DK Publishing, 2014.

INTERNET SITES

FactHound offers a safe, fun way to find Internet sites related to this book. All of the sites on FactHound have been researched by our staff.

Here's all you do:

Visit *www.facthound.com*

Type in this code: 9781491420164

 Check out projects, games and lots more at
www.capstonekids.com

INDEX